HERE COMES TROUBLE

NANCY WOLFE

PUBLISHED BY FASTPENCIL, INC.

Copyright © 2010 Nancy Wolfe

Published by FastPencil, Inc.
3131 Bascom Ave.
Suite 150
Campbell CA 95008 USA
(408) 540-7571
(408) 540-7572 (Fax)
info@fastpencil.com
http://www.fastpencil.com

No part of this publication may be reproduced, stored in a retrieval system, or transmitted, in any form, or by any means, electronic, mechanical, photocopying, recording, or otherwise, without the prior consent of the publisher.

The Publisher makes no representations or warranties with respect to the accuracy or completeness of the contents of this book and specifically disclaim any implied warranties of merchantability or fitness for a particular purpose. Neither the publisher nor author shall be liable for any loss of profit or any commercial damages.

First Edition

This book is dedicated to the two people in my life who have guided me the most: my mom and my husband.

Mom, throughout my whole life, you have always said I was the one who made you laugh. I have always just wanted to make you proud.

Jamie, all I can say is thank you. It takes a special kind of person to tough it out with me. I adore you.

Acknowledgements

First, I would like to acknowledge Jamie D. You helped build my confidence when I thought all of this was just foolishness.

Second, I would like to thank Marge. You were the final drop in the bucket.

Lastly, I want to acknowledge all the people who have told me, "You should write a book." Well, I did.

Contents

	Foreword	ix
Chapter 1	One	1
Chapter 2	Two	11
Chapter 3	Three	35
Chapter 4	Four	55
Chapter 5	Five	77
Chapter 6	Six	97
Chapter 7	Afterword	119

Foreword

*Whom God would sorely vex, He endows with
abundant good sense.*
-Yiddish Proverb

We all know someone who is unlucky. One of those pour souls who can never seem to outrun the dark cloud that follows them around no matter how hard they try; the proverbial "Schlep rock". There was a time in my life when I wouldn't believe such people actually existed, choosing rather to believe that these types were simply victims of their own impatience, inexperience, or incompetence. Over the last 17 years I have learned otherwise. I am pretty much convinced that certain people have an innate propensity for mishap. No, I am not one of these people, but I am married to one. My wife is not an airhead, dingbat or anything of the sort. We all make mistakes, have lapses in judgment and make poor decisions once in a while. This constitutes the lions' share of what we commonly refer to as "the human condition.", but some peoples' uncanny "ability" to become entangled in undesirable circumstances goes far beyond what bad luck or coincidence can explain away.

After living with Nancy and being caught up in her boundless mishaps for the better part of two decades I have learned a few things. Most importantly, the desire to overcome adversity is paramount for survival. Secondly, understanding and embracing your place in the universe and who you really are will bring clarity and sanity to your life. Finally, don't ever take yourself too seriously. Cling tightly to your sense of humor, as it will prop you up when nothing else can. Life is too short to sweat the small stuff, even when trouble comes calling.

1
ONE

"Among those whom I like or admire, I can find no common denominator, but among those whom I love I can: all of them make me laugh."

- W. H. Auden

I get my story telling ability from a long line of bullshitters. Of these, the two most notable are my mom and her mom, Grandma Kitty. Grandma Kitty would get to laughing so hard when telling a story, she would wet herself. She had so many stories- it is a shame she didn't write a book. Now HER life was an adventure. Mine? I'll call it a misadventure.

My Mom insists that her tombstone should read, "Here lies Patty. Her life was not boring." Next to that will be my tombstone, "Here lies her daughter, Nancy. Neither was hers." My favorite story my Mom tells involves false teeth, a knitted, hot pink bikini top, an inexperienced state trooper, and The Jesus Shoes.

The Jesus Shoes. There's so much about The Jesus Shoes that I can't even put it into words. These were the most God-awful sandals EVER. They were like prehistoric Jellies except not nearly as colorful, fashionable, or popular. The sandals were molded rubber with stamped indentations and ridges to make them look like real leather sandals. Oh Lord. Because adding that fine detailing made them that much more attractive. Sure.

Mom had a pair in dark tan and light tan because owning one pair of the ugliest shoes ever wasn't enough. Both pairs were speckled with paint splatters. THAT added to the fake detailing so nicely. Like every other kind of ugly shoes that have come along which people raved were *so* comfortable- Ugg boots, Crocs, Birkenstocks worn with socks- Mom insisted the sandals were *so* comfortable. Please- rocks would get stuck in the hollow parts of the heel. Walking with rocks in your shoes is as comfortable as wearing wet wool socks with Birkenstocks in the snow during cold winter months. I get it now.

Next, the false teeth. When Mom was in high school, one of her best buddies, Roger, thought it would be really funny to push her face down into the stream of water from the water fountain to get her face all wet. Unfortunately Roger misjudged his dunking abilities because he pushed her head too hard, causing her to knock out her four front teeth on the fountain nozzle. Ever since then, Mom has worn a plate to replace those teeth. Needless to say, the gap left between her teeth has been the topic of many off-color jokes. Use your imagination.

When I was little, we had one of those pull-out dishwashers that sat in the middle of the kitchen and was hooked up to the kitchen sink. It just so happened that said dishwasher was sitting out at the same time my mom had to sneeze. Out flew the teeth which hit the dishwasher and promptly broke. Of course, as with all well-timed emergencies, this was a Friday afternoon so she was unable to get into the dentist's office.

Now, for some reason, on Saturday morning when she got dressed to go the grocery store sans front teeth, Mom decided to pair The Jesus Shoes with cut-off jean shorts and this hand knitted, hot pink bikini top she had. And yes, the stitching was loose so, yes, things were showing that had no business showing. Keep in mind this *was* the seventies and Mom was pretty hot back in the day but, come on, a hot pink, hand knitted bikini top? To the grocery store?

So of course this was the perfect time for my Mom to speed down the highway because she hadn't quite called enough attention to herself yet in that outfit. And of course she got pulled over by a state trooper who looked as if it was his third day on the job.

What I would pay to have seen the look on the face of the state trooper when he walked up to our jalopy of a station wagon, with three young children riding in the back seat not wearing seatbelts with a woman wearing a top that barely qualified as clothing who smiled up at him with no front teeth. The poor guy probably figured if my mom could barely afford to dress herself and replace her teeth, she didn't have the money to pay a speeding ticket. After some stuttering and stammering, he let my Mom off with a warning about speeding. Mom went on her merry way. The officer was surely scarred for life.

That trooper probably still tells that story to his buddies. It's no wonder I grew up believing that embarrassment was one of my five senses.

***

I'm one of those people that things just happen to. I blame my Mom. For starters, she craved Limburger cheese when she was pregnant with me. Not cherry pie or pizza or some other food whose scent makes you smile when it wafts through the air. The scent of Limburger cheese doesn't waft delightfully through the air. It snatches you up and smacks you down. Secondly, she wasn't happy about being pregnant with her third child. My brother, Dan, wasn't quite four yet and my sister, Sandy, was barely 23 months older than me. All that negative energy was bound to affect me somehow. Add to that,

I flat out refused to eat them. Mom flat out refused to get me down out of the high chair until I had eaten them. And so began the first of many epic battles of wills between Mom and me. I sat there until the potatoes went cold. I sat there while everyone else finished dinner. I sat there after everyone had gotten down from the table. I sat there while Mom gave the angelic Dan and Sandy their baths. Finally, after she had tucked them into bed, she came to check on me (Hello? Children's Services? Anybody?). I had fallen asleep in the high chair, face down in the potatoes. Victory was mine.

***

Mom must have been a bigger sore loser than I first thought because she started plotting ways to "accidentally" ditch me.

The first incident occurred at my Grandma Wolfe's house. I was only about 6 months old. My Dad's side of the family had gathered for a nice family meal. When it was time to leave, everybody bundled up and loaded into the car. Mom was dreamily watching Divine Dan and

Saint Sandy riding next to each other so peacefully in the backseat, when, after they were more than halfway home, she started with a jump and yelled to my dad, "We forgot Nancy!" Forgot, my ass. Luckily, I was Dad's favorite so he immediately turned around and drove back to Grandma's house. When they got there, Mom tried to act all flustered like it was some kind of huge mistake that she felt just awful about. Grandma patted her on the shoulder and told her she knew they would have realized they had left me behind soon enough and would return for me. Don't bet on it, Granny.

It would have been one thing if that had been an isolated incident but it wasn't. When I was about five years old, we were once again visiting with the family only this time it was at our house. Mom and my Aunt Sarah decided that they would take the kids into town for ice cream. Yeah! Ice cream! Now this was back in the day when going to get ice cream was a rare treat. We were all so excited, especially me, because ice cream was my absolute favorite. So again, everybody loaded up, ignored any seat belts that may or may not have been available, and started off down the road. Once again Mom was checking on her precious Delightful Dan and Superb Sandy when she happened to look in the side rearview mirror. And there was poor little me running down the road after the jalopy, trying desperately to catch up. Mom says she still feels just awful about that and it still makes tears come to her eyes when she thinks back on me running as fast as my little legs could carry me.

Mom would have made an award winning actress, better than Joan Crawford even.

2

Two

"It's more satisfying to suffer the results of your own ideas than from someone else's."

- Unknown

Despite their reputations of being sooooo goooood, Mom used to get mad at Dan and Sandy because whenever I would get in trouble with her, they stick up for me, "Don't spank her, Mom," and then comfort me if I cried. Now Mom saw this as model behavior from her two darlings. Wrong. They were consumed with that good old Catholic guilt because most of the time they were involved in whatever trouble I happened to be in.

We grew up in the sticks surrounded by hills, woods, and a lake. For three kids whose mother's motto was "You'll live," it was a paradise. We swung on vines, ice skated, swam in the lake, drove go-carts with headlights made out of soup cans and candles so we could ride through the woods after dark, and rode our sleds stacked on top of each other like a Triple Decker bus to weigh the sled down more so that we could go airborne coming over the hills.

The winter after my traumatic ice cream incident, as soon as the lake had frozen over, we wanted to go skating but weren't allowed because Mom said the ice was too thin.

What did she know? Not as much as us, surely.

As soon as we got outside, Dan and Sandy decided that since I was the youngest, I was the one who should walk out on the ice to prove to Mom that she was mistaken. If Do-No-Wrong Dan said it was all right for me to go out onto the ice and Say-No-Evil Sandy agreed, and of course I knew I was right, then it MUST be okay. I didn't even make it past the end of the dock before that first heart-stopping, paralyzing crack sounded and reverberated across the ice. If you have ever been on ice, away from the safety of shore when it starts to crack, you know that feeling of fear. There is none like it. Before I could yell, "Oh, shit!" I fell through the ice.

Damn it! Mom was right.

Again.

This became the first of many times in my life when I realized that God has to like me because He always lets me get *this* close to dying without actually getting hurt.

At first, my fear was tempered with the fact that I wasn't alone in this. My brother and sister were with me after all. We were all in this together, weren't we? My visions of a brave and daring rescue quickly faded as Dan and Sandy just stood there. Hey guys, this is not the time to freeze up. I've got that covered pretty well right now.

It's a good thing that I was quite proficient at getting myself out of the trouble I got myself into because it was all up to me to haul my ass out of that lake and high tail it to the house soaking wet, freezing cold, not to mentioned scared stupid and just a little pissed off, looking for some comfort from the woman who was supposed to love me under any circumstances. If giving me comfort was in the form of a spanking, I was set for life. Man, could my Mom spank. Her favorite choice of weapon? Yep, you guessed it: The Jesus Shoes. She could whip those things off her feet and spank us faster than we could yell, "I didn't do it!" The rocks in the soles added to the velocity. It didn't matter how fast we tried to run past Mom or how much we were able to butt tuck, she always hit her mark. And she was right on target that day.

Then I got the standard, "If your brother and sister jumped off a cliff would you jump off too?" Of course! What fun would it have been standing safely on the edge of the cliff all by myself?

If the edge was actually safe, that is. There was one time when we were jumping back and forth over the drain ditch between the newly built foundation of a house and the bank surrounding it. Death-Defying Dan jumped with no problems. Super Sandy jumped with the greatest of ease. No such luck for Nancy.

When it was my turn to stand on the border of the dirt, just before I jumped, the edge gave way. I did manage to grab the outer corner of the foundation but my arms weren't strong enough to hold me. If I had just dropped, I might have walked away with only a few scratches, bruises, and hurt pride.

Not me.

Not one to admit defeat even when it is staring me in the face, I struggled to keep myself up even as I slid down along the corners of the concrete blocks. Just for the record, concrete blocks have very sharp edges. These managed to cut me open from my right hip bone diagonally across my torso to my left collar bone, leaving a nice jagged tear which left a scar I still have today. That sure was a fun walk home that day. Looking back now, I realize it was training for future events.

***

Don't get the wrong impression- we weren't hooligans. We really were good kids who loved our Mom and tried our best to listen. We were always trying to show her how much we loved her. When Sandy and I were little, we used to bring Mom bouquets of wildflowers- daisies, bachelor's buttons, goldenrod. We were always so impressed with how happy the flowers made Mom. They always brought tears to her eyes. We just thought all the sneezing she did was a cover up for her crying. Then there was the time Mom was at the grocery store and was running late. She called home and asked Dan to boil some eggs. Dan was more than willing to help out. Surely Mom would be thrilled when she finally dragged herself home after a long day to find a whole dozen eggs cracked into boiling water and left simmering in the pan for a couple of hours. Storming out of the house, muttering to herself about going back to the store which she had just left to buy another dozen eggs was a little confusing but again we thought she was trying get herself together and not show any more emotion than she already had.

At The Grocery Store was code for God, the Universe, and Miss Karma to huddle together and create divine inspiration. Everything always seemed to happen when Mom was At The Grocery Store. Mom was At The Grocery Store when a grouse flew through my bedroom window, crashed into the hall closet, and lay flapping around before it finally died covered in shards of broken glass. Mom was At The Grocery Store when I stepped on one of those hornets' nests that are in the ground and was immediately attacked and stung, like, a hundred thousand times. So it was natural that Mom was At The Grocery Store when I nearly cut my finger off after we received the inspiration to steal a street sign.

We had our sights set on a curves ahead sign. This particular curve sign didn't mark anything really dangerous. It stood at the top of Sells Road. Half of Sells Road was maintained by the city, which was tarred and chipped, and the other half was owned by the county, which was just gravel. Hardly anyone ever used this road and those that did already knew it was curvy. The way we saw it, why did they need a sign telling them something they already knew?

The plan was to ride our bikes to the top of Sells Rd. Sammy was the look-out person and I climbed up on Dan's shoulders to remove the sign. Now keep in mind that Dan's nickname when he was growing up was 'Ralph Ganorton, skinny little kid.' I used to tease him by asking him if he modeled for crucifixes- he was that bony and skinny.

There I was, trying to balance myself on Dan's shoulder bones and unscrew rusty nuts and bolts with no tools. The bottom bolt wouldn't budge but the top bolt loosened up easily. *Too* easily. Feeling overly satisfied with my handy work, I just knew another victory would be mine, if I could just figure out how I was going to get that piece of shi-

"CAR!"

Damn it! I was this close to successfully pulling off my first heist. Before I could react any further than that, Dan jerked backwards. I fell forward and caught myself by grabbing the sign post. This jolted the sign just enough to knock the top bolt loose.

It was then that I understood why utility workers always wear heavy work gloves. Everyone is always so concerned about playing with matches but no one ever warns to not play with street signs. That metal sign swung down like a pendulum blade and the corner of it sliced my finger to the bone. We were so in trouble now.

It's a funny thing about cuts that deep. They don't bleed right away like you'd think they would. Which didn't help because when we saw that flap of skin hanging open and my finger bone showing up white against the red of my flesh, we freaked.

Were we freaking about being arrested for stealing state property? No. Were we freaking that I might not have an index finger in the very near future? No. What we *were* freaking out about was what in the hell were we going to tell Mom?

As much as we loved Mom, we were afraid of her. Maybe it wasn't so much fear as it was respect. No- it was pretty much fear. But, we NEVER EVER wanted Mom to be disappointed in us either. Sacrificing a finger to keep Mom from finding out what had really happened was worth the price. I mean, this is the woman who was so mad at my dad for suddenly dying on her, leaving her a widow with three children ages 8, 10, and 12, that she buried him in a leisure suit.

A *rust-colored* leisure suit. With a dickie. If she was vengeful enough to doom my dad to spend eternity in one of fashion's worst polyester blunders and half a shirt, we could only imagine what she would bury us in after she killed us for trying to steal a street sign.

We were working under duress to think of an excuse because there was no way we were going to tell Mom the truth on this one. In a stroke of genius, a memory flashed through my head: a few years back I had wrecked on my bike and she had to use a needle to dig out rocks that had become imbedded in my forehead and the palm of my hand. Since Mom had been an actual witness to the aftermath of that bike ride, maybe she would believe us when we told Mom that I had wrecked on my bike and caught my finger in the spokes of the wheel. *That* was the brilliant story we invented after putting together such a genius plan of trying to steal a street sign in the middle of the day with no tools and using bikes as getaway vehicles.

How stupid did we think Mom was? That's just ridiculous right there.

Although, it wasn't a *complete* fabrication; I *had* been riding my bike.

You would think that coming from a large Italian family we would have been better at organized crime.

***

When people whom trouble is not a problem find themselves in a predicament, they are woefully unprepared with how to handle the situation. Growing up I found myself in enough predicaments, I considered myself a professional. My sister? Not so much. So when she did actually get in trouble for some minor infraction, and for my sister, minor was probably still too strong a word, it was a really big deal. So big, that it was, for some people (and you know who you are), hard to believe.

When Sandy was in the fifth grade and I was in the third, we had to ride the bus from St. Mary Elementary school, the school we attended, to East Elementary school, the school where my Mom taught. It was a short bus ride. Short enough that it was hard even for me to get into mischief besides the usual: staying seated, not being loud. For me, being loud is like breathing. So getting yelled at for yelling was no big deal.

There are some events in our lives that we never forget. The day my sister got loud with an adult is one that will play in my mind when I am on my deathbed and it will make me smile.

One major difference between my sister and I was that she loved school. I hated it. I used to get sick to my stomach every Sunday night during the school year. I hated it that much. So needless to say, getting out of school at the end of the day felt like a prison break.

There was just a short bus ride between me and total freedom.

One thing my sister and I did have in common was getting car sick. Swaying, bouncing school buses that reeked of diesel fumes were not meant to be ridden by people like us. I'm getting nauseous just thinking about it.

Sandy and I were sitting in the back of the bus. Okay, despite the fact that my sister graduated from college with a 3.9 GPA in mathematics and I have at least graduated from college, we weren't smart enough back then to figure out that sitting in the back of the bus wasn't the best idea for people who get motion sick. Being cool was more important and only dorks sat up front. Besides, our bus driver was a hag who smoked a lot, had a bad dye job, and listened to country music on a portable radio. Who wanted to sit next to that?

On this fateful day, it was raining. Raining hard. Raining hard enough to drip into the windows when they were pulled down. School bus design has always baffled me. The lack of seat belts, choking fumes, and windows that were always, always stuck which in turn led to pinched fingers by those stupid little buttons that needed to be pushed together to get the 'safety' Plexiglas to slide up and down is the stuff of childhood nightmares.

After pinching my fingers and getting soaked in the process, I managed to get the window down enough to get air blowing on our faces. For those of you who don't suffer from motion sickness, number one: be eternally grateful; number two: having air blow in your face or at least being able to stick a hand out the window and feeling the air on your fingertips helps immensely; and number three: you'll never be able to fully appreciate numbers one and two. Ms. Hag Busdriver must have been one of those non-motion sickness people because she started screeching at me to put the window back up, that it was raining, and I was getting the people behind us wet.

"Hey, stupid ass, we're sitting in the last seat, there isn't anyone behind us".

This is what I wanted to yell back at her but because I was a good Catholic girl, I yelled,

"No, they're not!" Whoa, calm down, Nancy, calm down.

Ms. Hag must have thought them was fightin' words because not only did she start shrieking back, she turned down her country music to do so.

Being car sick can have strange, detrimental effects because the next thing I knew, Sandy just lost it. She stood up out of her seat, told Hag to shut her damn mouth, and then flipped her off! I'm not talking about the 'stick a finger up behind the back of the seat so that it was half hidden' kind of finger flip. I'm talking about the in the air, in your face, 'what are you going to do about it' kind of finger flip. I had never been so proud of my sister before. It brought tears to my eyes. I just wanted to get out of my seat and yell, "That's right! That's MY sister!"

I got out of my seat, alright, just not the way I had envisioned it. No, I was thrown out of my seat when the bus driver, seeing my sister in the rearview mirror, slammed on the brakes, turned around in her seat, and started incoherently screaming at the top of her lungs. It was like a scene out of "When Pterodactyls Go Bad." I guess when a saint falls from grace, it brings out the worst in people.

I couldn't understand much of what Hag was yelling at Sandy but I did understand the gravity of the situation when she barked into her walkie-talkie that she was turning the bus around, returning to St. Mary's and kicking off my sister. Oh shit. Only hard core, troublemaking deviants got kicked off the bus. Hell, I hadn't even managed that one yet. MY SISTER WAS GETTING KICKED OFF THE BUS! Awesome! My chest was certainly swelling with pride at this point.

Back to the school we went, riding in oppressive silence. Sister Joanne, the principal, stood waiting for us with a scowl on her face that only a nun can wear. We dutifully followed her into her office, sat down, and waited for the axe to fall. Getting in trouble at school was one thing. As long as Mom didn't find out, it was tolerable. Getting in trouble at school and having Mom not only find out, but find out because the principal called? Atheists in foxholes didn't pray as hard as we did.

This was going to be my own private day of infamy. Not only was I so proud of my sister for her abrupt, blatant, disdain for authority, I was finally going to be vindicated for all the times I was the fall guy for her and Dan. For all the times I got yelled at and she didn't. For all the times Mom been unfairly harsher with me than the other two.

There IS a God.

But the Devil is in the details and he and I have hashed it out on several occasions.

Sister Joanne injudiciously put the screws to my sister by using speaker phone when she called Mom. I have to admit I was a little indignant at this. It was quite obvious that Sandy was a novice at getting in trouble because she was already crying, so why torture her even more by having to listen to my Mom morph into the banshee she became when she was mad? Sandy and I knew we were going to have to listen to Mom go on and on all evening about this ("And another thing, young lady....."). Mom doesn't know what 'let it go' means. There just didn't seem to be any point in getting her started any earlier than necessary.

The indignation I felt so smugly for my sister quickly turned personal when, after hearing Sister Joanne explain to Mom that Sandy had been kicked off the bus for flipping off the bus driver, Mom said, "You mean Nancy, not Sandy."

What?

Sister Joanne reiterated that yes, it was Sandy who was in trouble. To which Mom asked, "Are you sure it's Sandy, not Nancy?"

That's harsh.

***

Mom had good reason to question whether or not it was me who was in trouble at school. My infamy in school knew no limits. Mom had to attend many parent teacher conferences in which she was told, "Nancy certainty isn't like her brother and sister." I just don't think I was cut out for Catholic school.

First there was that scary thought of a 'calling.' The nuns explained that God could 'call' us into religious service as a nun or priest. This thought terrified me so much, I used to pray every night please, God, please, PLEASE don't make me a nun. What kind of sick mental torture were these nuns playing at?

Then there was the stairway incident during which I beat up Ted Slopeton when I was in the fourth grade. Well, damn it, he made my sister cry. This tendency toward violence followed me into middle school when I beat up Mike Oarwater. In my defense, I warned him three times to leave me alone. That's two times more than what he should have gotten but I really liked my teacher, Mr. Setter.

Next were the uniforms. I started a petition in the eighth grade to let the girls modify the uniforms by removing the tops of the jumpers. Then I started a petition in high school to make the boys have to wear uniforms. Oh they had a dress code – it consisted of dress pants of pretty much any color with a collared shirt- but it was not the same as the utterly horrible and restrictive, not to mention unfashionable, polyester uniforms the girls were required to wear.

Then I almost failed junior religion when, on the final exam, the essay question asked, "If you were the Pope, would you have supported President Reagan and his bombing of Libya?" See, here's the thing with Catholic schools: I received one hell of an education but they didn't always want to hear about it. I had the most inspiring history teacher, Mr. Trough. He had just given us a lecture on the whole Kaddafi-Libya-Reagan-defend-democracy thing (If you don't remember this incident in history, you are probably too young to be reading this book. You definitely grew up wearing a seat belt.).

Anyway, using the information Mr. Trough had given us, I wrote a beautiful essay explaining all the reasons why if I were the Pope I would have supported President Reagan. Father Douche failed me because the Pope would NEVER advocate violence in such a manner.

Well, what the shit, dude? You didn't ask *should* the Pope, you asked if *I* were the Pope and if *I* were the Pope, that's what I would have done. This led to another one of those parent/teacher conferences my mom had to suffer through. God bless her, she did take my side, which was a rare thing indeed, and managed to convince Father Douche that it was a well written essay (Thank you, Jesus, for letting my mom be a teacher too) and that if I were to fail religion class that year, he would have the pleasure of teaching me again the following year. I think I passed with a C.

My crowning moment though was when I got hit over the head with a Bible by my freshman religion teacher. Mr. Dork was a brand spanking new educator straight out of the seminary who had high aspirations of bringing God into the lives of young people. Oh please. God and I were already on a first name basis.

Religion wasn't high on my priority list of classes. I already had to go to church on Sundays, plus school masses on Wednesday. If I had spent that much time in a geography class, I would actually know where I am. So sitting in this guy's class listening to the same old 'this is how you should live your life' bullshit left me with plenty of time to think up ways to show my own unique individuality to Mr. Dork. I guess he didn't appreciate my efforts. His moment of losing total control in a fit of rage about some other thing I had done (See? It couldn't have been that bad, even I can't remember what it was that drove him over the edge) is another one of those deathbed memories: he grabbed a Bible off his desk, hit me over the head with it, and yelled,

"You ARE the devil!"

Thank God it was a soft bound version of the Bible or I might not have found the incident so hilarious. I can still see him coming at me in a sweater vest, arms raised above his head, sweat stains highlighting his armpits, eyes bulging, all red faced.

It was so funny.

When I was called into the principal's office to discuss the matter, I chose my favorite seat. I had had plenty of opportunities to test each chair in Father Paul's office and on my last visit to discuss my ingenious idea to pick the lock of the circuit box to turn off the clocks at lunch time so we could have a few more minutes of leisure time, I had decided that the third one from the window was the most comfortable. Plus it offered a great view. When Father Paul asked me what I had to say about the incident in Mr. Dork's class, I replied that it certainly gave new meaning to the term Bible thumper....

Mom thought the third seat from the window was comfortable too.

***

You gotta love Miss Karma, though. She will always get hers in the end: Ms. Hag Busdriver was later fired for picking up her friends and dropping them off at work while she had students on the bus. Ted Slopeton died of a drug overdose while working as a carnie. Mike Oarwater was arrested for impersonating a police officer. Mr. Setter was eventually promoted to principal. The boys now have to wear real uniforms not just dress pants and a collared shirt. Mr. Trough won Teacher of the Year several times. Father Douche was removed from his position after he was accused of molesting male students. It was all very hush-hush. Father Paul was promoted to the head of the diocese. As for Mr. Dork? He left teaching at the end of the year. I don't know what other fates he has had to face but I'm sure that hitting a student over the head with a Bible has to have some kind of consequence.

3

Three

"If at first you don't succeed, try, try again. Then quit. There's no use in being a damn fool about it."

- W.C. Fields

Through it all, my mom has repeatedly said that I was the one who always made her laugh. Yes, having a sense of humor has been my saving grace. It was also a good thing that I grew up thinking that being embarrassed was one of the five senses because it gave me lots of practice on how to save face when I became an adult.

Most especially when my engagement was broken off five weeks before my wedding.

Calling off a wedding that close to the date is like a massive product recall. It even feels like it has been announced on every news broadcast and in every newspaper. Since the invitations had already been sent out, the guests needed to be informed there had been a slight change in plans as quickly as possible. That meant calling each guest on the phone. The whole situation was bad enough but having to contact people in person? Ouch.

This was before email and text messaging so again, if you don't get that, put your seatbelt on.

I thought I was going to die of either a broken heart or embarrassment. Eventually embarrassment won out. At first I tried to be polite and politically correct in my explanation but after 4 or 5 calls, I lost my patience and just started to lay the truth right out there. It took a little longer, but it sure felt good.

Here's how it went down. I had lived with this guy, I'll refer to him as Dick, for about two years. We had set the wedding date soon after he graduated from college, *which by the way*, I helped pay for. We both worked for UPS; I worked the second shift, Dick worked the third shift. One evening I came home from work, tried on my wedding gown for the one hundredth time like all brides do, and saw the answering machine blinking. I had one new message.

"Hi Dick! It's Barry. Why don't you and Sheri join us at the bar for a drink?"

Sheri? When did I change my name to Sheri?

To give Dick the benefit of the doubt, I replayed the message to make sure I had heard it correctly. Yep, he definitely said Sheri. Suddenly all the suspicious happenings that Dick couldn't explain or explain sufficiently made sense.

There is nothing like discovering your fiancé's infidelity while standing in a wedding gown and wearing a veil while being called another woman's name. Man, was I pissed. And when I get pissed, you are going to know about it. Dick needed to know about it right then so I called him at work.

"What's up?" Dick asked oh-so-politely.

"Barry left a message for you. I think you need to hear it," was my icy reply.

You know what he said after I played the message for him? "That's a mistake." A mistake? No, a mistake is something you make when doing math. Being called by another woman's name on your own answering machine? That's a fuck up.

I told him he had 24 hours to come and get his stuff. After that, it was all going into the dumpster and the locks would be changed. He didn't believe me. Stupid little man. Twenty four hours later, his stuff was sitting in the dumpster and I was testing out my new door locks- and answering machine.

***

Ms. Karma must have felt sorry for me because if I had not dumped Dick when I did, I would have never been blessed with the love of my life, my husband, Jamie.

We met at the same UPS package center at which Dick and I met. He had just gone through a messy divorce and was still adjusting to life as a single parent of his then 2-year-old daughter, Chelsea. Here he was, a newly single, good-looking, intelligent man with a house of his own, a decent job, and the sympathy factor of having to raise a darling little girl on his own. He could have had anyone.

I still ponder over what it was about me that caught his eye. Was it my loud mouth booming over the noise of the machinery, telling dirty jokes to my all-male fellow employees or was it the appeal of my dirty clothes, worn steel toed work boots, and the lingering smell of sweat? I certainly didn't appear to be date material let alone a female role model/stepmother/wife and after my messy break-up with Dick I certainly didn't feel like female role model/stepmother/wife material.

Depending on whose point of view you're looking through, Ms. Karma must have been in a good mood that day or At The Grocery Store.

Still stinging from my latest disastrous relationship, I tried hard to be the Perfect Girlfriend. In being the Perfect Girlfriend, I was more enthusiastic about certain activities than I normally would have been. Hunting, fishing, and camping were some of the activities Jamie wanted to share with me. Jamie is the epitome of the Outdoorsy Type. He is devoted to hunting. Not just hunting but hunting with traditional equipment-wooden bows he has made by whittling down an Osage Orange stave and wooden arrows he made by gluing knocks, feathers, and arrow heads onto them. He has hunted and fished around the world. All of his friends hunt and fish. His phone conversations are about hunting and fishing or preparing to go hunting and fishing or the next hunting and fishing trip or rehashing previous hunting and fishing excursions. Our house is fashionably decorated with various stuffed fish, deer heads, deer skulls, deer antlers, bows, arrows, as well as pictures of him holding dead deer or fish, or framed prints that incorporate all of the above mentioned items. I think the only reason why he stuck with me is because I was the only woman he dated who, while making out with him on the couch and opening my eyes only to have a dead deer staring down at me, didn't run immediately run out of the house.

Along with Catholic school, hunting, fishing, and camping are activities that I was not cut out for. I don't like bugs. I don't like being hot. I don't like waking up early. I don't have patience. I can't stand still and be quiet at the same time. Killing something is too much responsibility.

Fish scare me and I feel sorry for the worms. Lastly, since the invention of the bed spring, there is no reason for anyone to have to actually choose to sleep on the ground. So you can see why being the Perfect Girlfriend was very difficult for me. I had a lot working against me.

My big fishing and camping debut happened at Seneca Lake. It was the hottest weekend of the summer. I'm talking in the mid to upper nineties with matching humidity levels. It was also peak mosquito season. Despite repeating to myself, "This is going to be fun. This is going to be fun," I knew it was going to be hell on earth for me.

Still trying to be Perfect Girlfriend, I dutifully got up before dawn, put on my hot neon orange bikini (like mother, like daughter?), helped Jamie back the boat in the water, and commenced to spending many, many, *many* fun-filled hours standing in the back of the boat, huffing gasoline fumes, slapping at mosquitoes until the sun came up and then starting to slowly bake in the withering heat under a glaring sun in a cloudless, windless sky. Oh the joy.

Finally I had enough. I was bored out of my skull and was suffering from heat stroke and motion sickness. I was just about to tell this to Jamie when he hooked a fish. It was a hog- a large mouth bass weighing over four pounds and was 22 inches long. Jamie was in his glory, wrangling in this fish.

"Get the net! Get the net!" he yelled at me, still pulling and reeling in his line. When I handed it to him he said, "No, no. Get down on the floor, lean over the side of the boat, and put the net in the water as deep as you can. I don't want the fish to see it. When I bring him in, scoop him up in the net from as far underneath him as you can. I don't want to spook him."

Me get down on the dirty boat floor in my cute little neon orange bikini? *Me* lean over the side of the boat and scoop up the fish? Oh no. And why was the fish's fear of more concern than mine?

Arguing was out of the question because by now Jamie's shouting had attracted the attention of the people on the shore and they were all watching us. Please, dear God, do NOT let one of my boobs pop out of this bikini top in front of all this people, I fervently prayed.

For once God answered my prayers. He didn't let me embarrass myself by having a wardrobe malfunction. Oh no. God had a more amusing way for me to embarrass myself in front of half the population of Seneca county.

I was leaning so far over the boat my face was inches from the water. I had the net so far down into the water, my whole arm was submerged. I was patiently waiting to see the fish swim by so I could gracefully scoop him out of the water and finally attain Perfect Girlfriend status when this gigantic, monstrous fish came shooting up from the depths of the lake, its mouth wide open, teeth glittering in the scorching sun, and jumped out of the water, right into my face. I can still see the look of murder in that fish's eyes. I'm telling you, if I hadn't fallen back into the boat, screaming at the top of my lungs that the fish was trying to bite my head off, that fish would have bit my head off.

As Jamie glared down at me and snatched the net off the boat floor, I knew that in one swish of its spiny tail, that fish just ruined my chances of ever being Perfect Girlfriend.

Perfect Girlfriend or not, Jamie still married me. And he loves telling this story.

***

I am a hard head. One would think I should have just given up on fishing. But nooo, I just couldn't let it go. Continuing my efforts to be Perfect Girlfriend, I agreed, again, to go fishing with Jamie and his uncle, The Goof. I was still suffering from Post Traumatic Stress Disorder as a result of my being attacked by the large mouth bass but Jamie assured me that these were *small* mouth bass and didn't grow to be as sizeable as the one at Seneca Lake. My anxiety increased when I realized that I had to wear waders. If I was worried about my ass looking big in a pair of jeans, I was mortified at how I looked in the waders. I decided that the hot orange bikini hadn't brought me much luck so what the hell, they were wearing waders too.

All was going well. I hadn't caught a thing. But neither had they so we headed down stream into deeper water. Jamie and The Goof were ahead of me because waddling in waders required way more skill than I first thought and I was having some serious difficulties.

As they were crossing the creek, I watched as the water rose higher and higher on their chests.

Both of them are well over 6 feet tall and I am 5'9" on a good day. I knew there was no way in hell that I was tall enough to cross where they were crossing. The both of them were in some deep conversation involving deer or deer hunting or deer hunting clothes or deer hunting spots or dead deer or deer that should be dead and they weren't paying a bit of attention to me which was all fine and good up till now because I was about as unsexy as I could have been in those damn waders. Plus I was sweating. But now I needed Jamie's attention.

"Jamie, honey, I'm not tall enough to cross here."

Without even glancing my way he replied "Yes you are." And continued on with his conversation about the same damn deer stories they have told each other a hundred times. They already knew how each story ended but got just as excited with each retelling.

"Jamie, really, I can't make it across. Should I go upstream a little ways?"

"So I see this deer sneak in. He was facing me at an angle, 20 degrees west-south-west and the wind was blowing from the north at 5 miles an hour...."

"Guys, really, I don't think I can make it across."

Nothing.

Now I was starting to get annoyed. When I get annoyed, I get pissed off. So with an I'll-show-you attitude, I waded into the river and sure enough that water started rising higher and higher up my chest. When it reached the very top of my waders, I again tried to get some help,

"JAMIE! The water is too deep. Help me."

Nothing again.

Oh for God's sake, the deer was already dead and had been for 5 years. I was going to be dead if I couldn't get him to understand that I was literally getting in over my head.

"Jamie, Help me!"

"You're fine. Don't get the fishing pole wet."

Don't get the fishing pole wet? Fishing poles are made to be used in the water. That's where the fish live- in the water. What the hell?

I found this nonsensical male logic idiotically funny so I started laughing. As soon as I started laughing, the water started seeping into my waders. The more the water tipped into my waders the funnier I found the situation to be. Pretty soon, I was laughing so hard the water just gushed into the waders, pulling me down until just my head was above water. But by God, I had that fishing pole above my head, making sure *it* was safe.

This whole time, I am still trying to get Jamie's attention although by now I was gasping for air due to my hysterics and sputtering water out of my mouth. Jamie and The Goof were already walking along the shore, at least 10 yards ahead of me and did either one of them turn around to see if I really needed help? Hell no.

I began to have visions of me being swept away, never to be heard from again. That is until Jamie sees his pole floating in the water and starts looking around for me so that he can give me the lecture on how I need to take better care of his fishing poles only to find I was nowhere in sight. Once again, I was left with only myself to rely on, so I shimmied my way out of the sunken waders, and dragged them and myself to shore.

Man, was I pissed off!

I went off on a classic Mom Tirade, all the while trying to dump wet sand out of my sopping socks. I finished my tantrum with the announcement that I was going back to the truck and stalked off- well, stalked off the best I could. Wet waders are even harder to walk in than dry ones.

There were only two times during our courtship that I seriously considered ending the relationship and this was one of them. Like I said, I am a hard head and do not give up easily. It's a good thing too. Just think how dull Jamie's life would have been without me.

**

Albert Einstein famously defined insanity as doing the same thing over and over again but expecting different results. You would think by now that I would have learned my lesson and avoid fishing or using waders. Not so.

If I were given the opportunity to meet any three people in the world, Cesar Millan would be my number one choice. The Dog Whisperer knows his stuff. I try my best to do it Cesar's way at home with my two yellow Labrador Retrievers,

Lewis and Clark. Sometimes I am a successful pack leader, sometimes I am not.

I decided I needed to channel as much pack leader mentality as I could muster in trying to cure Lewis of a sudden fear of – me. It started one morning as we were walking up the stairs. Because it was time for breakfast and Lewis always acts as if he's starving, he was enthusiastically bounding up the stairs in front of me when suddenly he yelped, lifted his back left leg, and hobbled up to the landing. When he turned to face me, he had this look on his face as if to say, "What did you do to me? That HURT!" Doing it Cesar's way, I didn't baby him or try to pet him. I told him to go on up the stairs, with the intention of calming him down and checking out his leg once we were clear of the stairs.

I was being a calm, assertive pack leader. Lewis saw things differently- he thought I was being Satan's right-hand man and poking him with a sharp stick. From that point on, for about a month, Lewis ran in the opposite direction when he saw me coming. It really hurt my feelings not to mention how inconvenient it became because I'm pretty much the caregiver for the dogs; I feed them, exercise them, clean up after them. All that fun stuff that pet ownership entails.

In one of my favorite *Dog Whisperer* episodes, Cesar flies to Florida to work with a yellow lab named Jake. To gain the trust of the dog, he donned a wetsuit, got in the owners' pool, and spent the afternoon letting Jake float on his back while Cesar held him. It was so cool the way he got the dog calmed and relaxed. The look on Jake's face as he floated in Cesar's arms was so serene, I decided I could do the same thing with Lewis. Except we don't have a pool- we have a pond. A pond in which the edges quickly drop off to 15 feet deep. And it wasn't sunny Florida in the summertime- it was autumn in Ohio. Not to mention the lack of a wet suit. Wet suit? Who needs a wet suit? I have waders.

Never mind all that- I am the pack leader and I need to lead my dog past his fear of me. So dunking him in a cold pond while I sloshed around in my waders was exactly what he needed, he just didn't know it yet.

After working my way into the infamous waders, I convinced Lewis to follow me out to the pond to 'Go Swim'. Besides 'Let's Eat', 'Go Swim' is his favorite command. I let him hobble his way into the water and swim around a little bit before claiming the pond as mine by stepping in and walking out as far as I could before I reached the drop off. Normally, the water would have been at least 5 feet deep where I was standing but since Ohio had been in a drought that summer, the water level was low. This meant I was standing on a slope rather than flat ground. That didn't concern me in the least. I just squatted down and pulled Lewis over to me.

I mimicked Cesar's every move- I took deep breathes to calm myself and Lewis. I sat him in my lap to let him adjust to being held in the water, and then I flipped him onto his back.

Holy shit! It worked! Lewis was just as calm and tranquil as could be. Both of us began to really enjoy the moment when slowly, oh-so-slowly, my feet began to slide in the mud. I didn't want to make any sudden moves and spook Lewis so I tried to take a step back. But, just like in the creek, water started draining into my waders, pulling me forward. I knew the edge of the drop off had to be dangerously close but I didn't want to ruin the mood for Lewis or show any weakness as the pack leader, so, as I started sliding deeper into the water, I gently raised him higher and higher until finally he was literally laying on my head while I frantically tried to get my feet back under me.

There are times when I know God is watching me and laughing his ass off. I just know He was up there, calling over to his buddies, "Come here! Come here! You gotta see this!" Here I was, in a pond, wearing waders, holding a dog on my head, with my feet stuck in the mud, trying not to go under water, all the while thinking that I was a pack leader.

Since I amuse myself to no end, I started laughing at myself and the absurdity of the situation which, again, created just enough movement to get the water gushing into the waders. This time my luck ran out. With one last ditch effort, I tried to reverse my momentum but ended up losing my balance and slid off the shelf on the pond edge and was quickly sucked under. I was once again amazed at how fast waders can fill with water. I was also amazed at how hard it is to laugh under water no matter how ridiculously funny the situation may be. I just remember looking up from below the surface, and seeing the serene look of content on Lewis's face as he floated on his back and thinking to myself that this is not how things turned out for Cesar. Lewis must have connected with my new found lightheartedness and realized that I really wasn't the devil poking him with a stick because he rolled himself over and swam to shore. The upside of having waders fill up fast, if they're not being worn in fast moving water, once they fill, they are easy to get out of but heavy as hell to drag out.

I had to do it though. Jamie had bought the waders for me and I didn't want to disappoint him by letting them sink to the bottom of the pond. I could just hear him in my head, "What? You got the waders wet?"

After lugging the waders out of the pond, I joined Lewis on the bank where he lavished me with kisses and tail wags. Sitting there on the bank of the pond, enjoying the moment with one of my best buddies, taking in the crystal clear blue sky, the slanted rays of the sun reflecting off the surface of the pond, I realized life is truly what you make it and I would really like to make mine a lot easier.

4

Four

"It's better to burn out than fade away."

- Neil Young

If fire is the Devil's only friend then I must be one of his very close relatives. My friends don't call me the Devil; they call me Sparky. Yup, I've had that many showdowns with fire. I can't intentionally start a fire to save my life but catch a compost pile on fire in the middle of January with a foot of snow on the ground? Now that's a skill.

I first discovered this natural ability of mine when, feeling guilty about leaving behind a large carbon footprint by burning wood in the winter to heat the house, I decided to give back by salvaging the ashes and add them to the compost pile. Reduce, reuse, recycle!

Now, to my credit, I know better than to just dump a pail full of hot ashes onto anything, so after emptying the stove, I let the bucket sit outside on a stepping stone for 2 days- in January- in the snow- for 2 whole days. What more did I possibly need to do to get that damn thing cooled?

So, because the ashes had been sitting in 20 degree weather with accumulating precipitation on and around the bucket, I felt it safe to dump the ashes onto the compost pile. One of the very few advantages of the cloudy, grey, gloomy, dark, dull days of Ohio winters is that anything lighted, or glowing, or bright, sticks out like, well, a glowing ember. So again, to my credit, as I poured the ashes out, I was watching for any red coals that could have still been hot. Nothing. Since it had started snowing again, I felt it was safe to go inside to my nice, warm, fossil fuel burning house and relax for the evening.

That lasted about an hour when Muttley, my black Lab, started barking and whining, running from the bedroom to the family room where I was lounging with not a care in the world. Muttley on the other hand, looked like he was going to have a stroke if I didn't get up and follow him. I needed to pee so I figured I might as well get up and see what was aggravating him.

As I walked into the darkened bedroom, I could see a strange flicking light dancing on the walls. Stepping up to the french doors, I saw the source of this light and it wasn't dancing- it was flames shooting into the evening sky from the compost pile! Now normally I wouldn't have panicked. Compost piles need to get "hot" so that the plant material can break down. But I since I had built the compost pile up against a utility pole that was soaked in flammable creosote, I figured I had better get my lounging ass out there.

Again, in my defense, I thought I had thoroughly contemplated the location of the compost bin. I built it against the utility pole for two very logical reasons. First, the pole is at the edge of the garden so I could easily throw in any garden waste and, just as easily, shovel the composted matter into the garden when I needed it. Second, by building it next to the pole I only had *one* big thing to mow around instead of two, smaller, annoying things. It seemed like a good plan at the time.

As I was rushing to put on my boots and a coat, I decided it might be a good idea to get Jamie. He rarely panics and almost always has a solution to a problem. He was in the garage/workshop building a bow (there's a shocker) with his buddy, Brian.

I ran to the garage, threw open the door, grabbed a shovel while yelling, "Jamie, I need your help! The compost pile is on fire!" I thought that was sufficient explanation. Unfortunately, they couldn't understand what I had said. As Brian tells it, they saw me run in, knock around some garden tools, yelling, "BLAH-BLAH, blah blah blah blah! Blah blahblah blah blah FIRE!" He looked at Jamie and asked, "Did she just say FIRE?" They both looked out the window, saw me running across the yard, saw the fire (which by now had grown despite the wet conditions), and decided to grab shovels too. There we were, shoveling snow onto the burning compost bin, hoping like hell the utility pole didn't catch fire. Not one of my more stellar moments.

The score: Me =1. Fire=0.

Round Two was another test of how close to dying I could get without being hurt. The house we bought in was build by the owner in 1982. He either didn't know what he was doing or he didn't care if it was done right. We have uncovered enough of his scarily botched handiwork that it has woken me up at night in a cold sweat.

I have, over the years, improved the landscaping immensely. One of my first projects was to move a group of hosta plants out back. I spent most of the day outside because I really wanted to get them all moved as soon as possible because it was supposed to rain that evening. I worked my ass off, digging new holes, adding my freshly toasted compost (despite the charred bits, it was rather nice), and moving the plants. When I did finally take a break, it was a short one because the electricity had gone off for about an hour. Because the house wasn't built according to any legitimate building code I'm aware of, the electricity went off a lot. Just my luck. I was dying of thirst, needed to pee, as usual, and couldn't do either. Oh well, I thought, this will keep me from lollygagging. So I went back to work.

I was so proud of myself when I finished. Up until that point of my life, I was really only good at two things: gardening and baking. Satisfied that my new flower bed would be beautiful, I went inside just as the rain started to fall.

Well, my smug satisfaction didn't last very long. As soon as it started to really rain hard, the lights started to flicker while making a very unsettling sizzling sound. I'm no electrician but when my lights start making spitting and hissing sounds, I know there is a problem somewhere. While Jamie checked the breaker box, I noticed that one of my hostas was smoking. I'm no master gardener either but when my plants start smoking…

"Jamie, honey, I think I see part of the problem," I stated as matter-of-factly as I could, trying to be nonchalant so as to not get him wound up any more than I knew he would be. Like with Mom, I saw no need to get him started any sooner than possible. "I think my hosta plant is on fire."

If seeing a burning compost pile shoot flames 15 feet into the air while it was snowing had been an odd sight, there's nothing like seeing a flower bed full of green hostas spewing smoke during a rain shower. By the time we got our boots on, found shovels (I have since moved the shovels to an easy-to-reach location right inside the garage door), and made it back to the flower bed, there was a patch of scorched and smoldering dirt the size of a basketball. Who knew dirt can actually burn?

Without realizing it, I had cut the electrical line from the house to the garage with the shovel while digging up the plants. When it started to rain, the moisture seeped into the casing, causing the electricity to flicker while melting the dirt into a Chernobyl mess.

Upon further inspection, Jamie discovered that the wires had been buried less than 12 inches deep. So see, I'm really not the source of the many problems I have created. It's just God getting in a good belly laugh at my expense. God bless Him, though, He planned that power outage just right.

    The score: Me=2; Fire=0.

My next adventure with my good friend Fire can again be chalked up to me trying to avoid a potential disaster only to find myself in the middle of it. Our friend Rodney had helped us build a deck/screened in porch on the back of our house. In return, I agreed to mow his lawn for the summer. I'm one of those freaks of nature who actually enjoys mowing, especially if I get to use a riding mower or lawn tractor. I put in my earbuds, pop on some earmuffs, fire up the tractor, and sing to my heart's content without having to worry about anyone hearing me over the noise of the tractor.

The one yard chore I do not do any more, under any circumstances, is trim. I have hacked down or into way too many flowers, shrubs, trees, toads, siding, and hoses. I have soundly learned that there are some gardening chores that are better left to someone else. Trimming is one. Stacking firewood is another. So when Rodney insisted I trim his yard in addition to mowing, even Jamie came to my defense when I refused. Rodney wouldn't hear any of it.

"You can't be that bad at trimming. Your yard always looks nice. Besides, I have a brand new trimmer in the garage you can use." After several more minutes of protesting, I finally agreed to trim his yard with the warning that I would not be responsible for any loss of life or property. Rodney just chuckled, thinking I was exaggerating. Another silly man.

The fateful day arrived. I drove over to Rodney's and was going to retrieve his trimmer when I discovered he had locked it in the garage and hadn't left me a key. This should have been the first sign to leave it alone. But no, I had given my word that I would mow and trim his yard so that was what I was going to do. I drove back home and got our trimmer.

Now since I do not trim at our house, under any circumstances, I didn't realize that Jamie had replaced the string with a blade that he uses to cut down the brush at the edge of our property. At that time, the trimmer was newly in our possession and I wasn't familiar with it. To me, everything seemed in order because that is how Jamie was using the trimmer the last time I saw him with it.

Back at Rodney's, I was being oh-so-careful with the trimmer. First, it was new and Jamie would be really pissed off if I broke his very expensive Stihl trimmer. Secondly, I knew my limitations when operating such equipment. I have yet been allowed to use the chainsaw. So when I started trimming, I was moving very deliberately and slowly. I worked in very small sections, one section at a time. I trimmed the edge of his edging. I trimmed around the decorative rocks. I trimmed around the hostas (another omen?). I trimmed around the corner of the house until I came to his air conditioning unit.

Oh shit. An electrical appliance.

I located the wiring and any other parts that could be dangerous if accidentally hacked into and again started to slowly, slowly, work my way around the unit. I was so focused on the air conditioner that I was caught completely off guard when I heard a SCRAP-WHOOSH-HISS noise. What the hell is that, I thought to myself as the hissing sound grew louder and more incessant. I was so focused on not hitting the air conditioner that I didn't see the gas pipe. I had just cut Rodney's gas line in half and gas was spewing out.

I admit it. I panicked. Here I was holding a power tool fueled by gasoline, which was still running by the way, standing right next to a cut gas line. I am always amazed at the situations I find myself in. Because I knew I was panicked, I was trying not to act panicked. I carefully backed away from the freshly severed pipe and then ran like hell to the driveway to my car to get my cell phone.

Because we live in the sticks, signal strength for cell phones can be spotty at best so I spent what felt like an eternity repositioning myself to find a signal strong enough to call 911. It was embarrassing enough to have to explain what I had done but when the operator asked for the address, I had to tell her I didn't know; that I would have to run to the end of Rodney's driveway and look on the mailbox.

"You don't know the address?" she asked incredulously, "I thought you said this was a friend of yours." Look lady, I just know where he lives, not the specific coordinates.

Because I was huffing and puffing my way down the driveway and didn't answer her right away, she asked again, "You really don't know where your friend lives?"

"Yes, I know where he lives," I shouted into the phone. "He lives 2 miles down the road from us! And no, I don't know his phone number either!" Like every other modern day person, all of this information is saved in my phone. To retrieve it I would have had to hang up, look up Rodney's contact information, and call 911 back. Since I had a hard enough time getting service in the first place, I felt it was vital for me to cling to this connection.

And again, because we live in the sticks, we don't have a regular fire department. The Hartford Fire Department is all volunteer, made up of local farmers and other hard working citizens who, when called to an emergency, have to stop what they're doing and respond. These are people I will be seeing at the grocery store, gas station, bank, and on trick-or-treat night. Hell, even my neighbor across the road is one of the volunteer firefighters. This wasn't going to be one of those mortifying experiences in which I could make myself feel better by saying, "Oh well. I looked like a jack ass but I'll never see these people again." Yeah, this fun-filled lawn care experience was going to be painfully awkward. It was made even more awkward when the fire department showed up in their bomb suits, just in case there was an explosion.

"Oh, hello, Mr. Morris. How are you today?" I asked, trying to sound, calm, cool, and collected.

"What seems to be the problem?" he asked.

"Well, I kinda cut through the gas line."

"Kinda cut?"

"Okay. I cut right through the damn thing. I was trying to avoid the air conditioner and didn't see the pipe," I explained, trying to sound as much like a man as possible because I was trying desperately to not sound like a woman who had just pulled some kind of non-man, bonehead move, only to have this group of manly men staring at me like I'm a woman who just pulled a non-man, bonehead move. I was grasping at straws. I fleetingly thought of lowering the neckline of my tank top and sticking my boobs out but since I'm not what you would call well-endowed, I knew from past experiences that that wouldn't work. That's when I noticed several of the men admiring the trimmer. I figured I could use that as a distraction tool when one of them looked up and asked, "Is that a Stihl?"

"Yes, it is." I answered, thinking I was cool enough to be one of the guys because I had a really cool piece of equipment.

"Is it new?"

"Yes, it is," I said standing up a little straighter, a little taller, a little less embarrassed.

"Is it your husband's?"

"Yes, it is," I responded, proud that I had a husband who used only the best tools.

"Does he know you're using it?"

Reality had finally snapped me out of it by slapping me upside the head, reminding me that I was not the he-woman I wanted to be, only a boneheaded woman who had nearly blown up my friend's house with a power tool. My deflated ego dragged my sorry ass back to the car and out of their way while they repaired the gas line, packed up their equipment, and with a pitiful shake of their heads, left me standing in the driveway, wondering how I was going to explain this to Rodney. More importantly, I was wondering how I would be able to convince Jamie to let me use his tools again. He really does have cool stuff.

The score: Me=3, Fire=0.

Round Four also involved a power apparatus. One of my favorite pieces of equipment Jamie owns is the leave blower. The one he has is a beast. It's like a backpack and can peel the paint off of a house so blowing leaves and/or clearing the sidewalk is usually a breeze.

Because of the direction of the wind, blowing leaves at our house is tricky. I have it down to a science. I have learned how to play the wind in my favor, corralling the leaves into the garden to be used as compost. I compost the leaves instead of sending them off to the landfill to (again) counteract the damage to the environment I cause when I burn a small pile. Unlike the carbon footprint I create by burning wood to heat the house in the winter, I don't burn enough leaves to create an actual footprint. It's barely a toe print but just the same, composting leaves helps the gardener in me feel better. I know it is against the law in most areas and bad for the environment but, like fresh cut grass in early summer, there is just nothing like the smell of burning leaves on a cool, crisp autumn evening when the days are getting shorter, the sunlight is getting weaker, and The Ohio State Buckeyes are playing in the Horseshoe. I feel sorry for the seatbelt wearing/texting/twittering/Wii playing generation who will never know what it is like to have that wonderful smell drifting through the air while trick-or-treating in the dark. Being politically correct sure has taken the fun out of a lot of things. But I digress.

Like I said, I like to burn a pile or two just for the pure fun of it. Trickier than blowing the leaves into the garden is to get the leaves in a neat pile close to the fire ring because the wind usually blows out of the west, across the ring, out over the pond. See, this was good thinking on my part in planning the position of the fire ring. It's not close to anything that could naturally be set on fire, like the utility pole, but close enough to the pond in case my Fire Starter skills sneak up on me and something does actually catch on fire and needs to be put out quickly. This is especially important in the fall during hunting season because Jamie is in and out, heavy on the out, so if I would ever need his help, he probably won't be around.

So on a beautiful autumn day, I wrangled with the leaves and in record time, cleaned up the yard. As a reward, I decided to have a little fire out by the pond and enjoy the rest of the day listening to the Buckeyes' game on the radio.

I was feeling a little cocky. I was very proud of the two neat stacks of leaves I had created: compact, tidy, and on the opposite side of the fire pit, out of the wind. I had started the fire on the first try, using only scraps of firewood so as to not use our high-quality firewood. And the best part was the Buckeyes were winning.

I got my lounger out of the garage and positioned it just right, not too close to the fire and angled so I had a fantastic view of the pond and the woods, next to the radio with the antennae touching the metal legs to improve the reception of the football game. I got the dog blankets from the laundry room and spread them out next to the lounger. All I had left to do was make myself a nice, tall, refreshing gin and tonic and go to the bathroom, as per usual.

As I carefully navigated the steps with drink and snack in hand, Lewis and Clark started barking and whining, running from the bedroom to the bottom of the steps where I was already dreaming of my imminent lounging with not a care in the world. Lewis and Clark on the other hand, looked like they were going to have a stroke if I didn't pick up the pace and follow them. As I walked into the darkening bedroom, I could see a strange flicking light dancing on the walls. ….Hmmm. This was weird. It felt like I had already lived this moment once before….

Stepping up to the french doors, I saw the source of this light and it wasn't dancing- it was flames shooting from the inferno created by my first nice, tidy, compact pile of leaves! With Fritos flying and Tanqueray trickling down my hand, I ran out of the house and down to the fire pit to see what in the hell was going on. There was no way this could have happened. I was so careful about everything: placement of the leaves, assessment of the wind direction, containment of the small fire, and putting away the lighter fluid. I had done *everything* with safety in mind.

By some total freak of nature, the wind had suddenly shifted directions and was blowing straight out of the east, something it RARELY does at our house. Even when it did, it would be blocked by the woods, diminishing its strength. Not this time. Oh no, it was skimming right across the pond, allowing the flames to lick at the edges of the leaves which of course went up like the Hindenburg. The more I tried to stamp out the fire, the more the wind blew.

It was like in the movies when Bruce Willis or some other action hero lays down a line of gasoline and sets it on fire. As it shoots across the asphalt, the bad guys scramble to get out of the way before the line of fire reaches its intended target and with an air-sucking whoosh, creates a massive, screen-filled fireball. It was just like that except the fire was following a line of leaves from the first pile to the second pile while I was scrambling to get the rest of the leaves out of the way. It was no use. As the line of fire reached the second pile of leaves, in one breathtaking whoosh, it created a massive, sky-filling fireball. By the time I filled two five-gallon buckets of water from the pond, it was over, leaving a huge area of the yard scorched, and seared, shriveled leaves and twigs dropping from the nearby maple tree.

Oh good Lord. Sometimes I really do get tired of trying to explain myself.

The score: Me=4, Fire=0.

Ah, but as everyone knows, if you play with fire, just as with Satan himself, eventually you will get burned. God and Miss Karma must have been At The Grocery Store, allowing Fire to score one. One a cold January day we lost everything in a house fire, including my dogs at the time, Jack and Murphy. Poor Murphy. I had rescued him from the dog shelter just eight weeks earlier after having to put Muttley down in October. If I had not adopted Murph, he might still be alive today. Talk about guilt.

I cannot think about losing Jack without getting choked up. He was my first dog as an adult. He was smart, friendly, and beautiful. He was my best buddy. I will never forgive myself. That dog would have walked to Hell and back for me and I wasn't there when he needed me the most.

Jack was the best dog ever.

Four

I'm pretty sure the fire was my fault because I was the last to check the wood burning stove before everyone left for the day. The experience nearly crushed me. That's all I got to say about that.

5

Five

"I came. I saw. I conquered."

- Julius Caesar

I am culinarily challenged. Saying I am culinarily challenged might even be an understatement. Ask me to paint a room or create a whole garden from seed- no problem. Ask me to cook anything more complicated than grilled cheese and tomato soup and that is asking for disaster. My only redeeming quality in the kitchen is my baking skills. Unfortunately, my reputation in the kitchen is so tarnished not many people believe I have this skill, even after eating one of my homemade desserts. Who can blame them after I set a sheet of meringue cookies on fire in the oven? Needless to say, I feel I have a lot to prove.

Not one to shy away from a challenge, I decided to enter one of my specialties, White Chocolate Cream Cheese Filled Chocolate Cupcakes, in the baking contest at the Hartford Fair. Since the fair is known as the "biggest smallest county fair," I just assumed the baking contest would fall into the smallest category.

I just knew I had this one in the bag. It's the Hartford Fair- how hard could it be to win? I hadn't even baked the cupcakes yet and I was already claiming bragging rights. I was so confidant, I started shooting my mouth off to other fairgoers. That's always a good idea.

Imagine my surprise when I showed up with my five cupcakes on a chipped nacho plate and was thrown into one of the biggest competitions at the fair. I could not believe the number of entrants. I could not believe the number of entries. I could not believe the level competition. There were bakers that had competed in this contest for decades. Many of these were consistent winners. Newcomers were pooh-

poohed away by these veterans. It was assumed the same people would win year after year.

Because they usually do.

At the sudden loss of my confidence, I positioned myself in the very back of the room closest to the door so that when I came in dead last, I could make a swift, albeit humiliated departure.

After four hours of waiting in embarrassment (what *was* I thinking, entering a contest that involved the use of a kitchen?), the judges had made their final decisions. Third place was announced. I backed up to the door a little more. Second place was announced. My hand was almost on the door handle. A palpable silence engulfed the room as everyone held their breath waiting for the announcement of the grand prize winner.

"And first place goes to…..Nancy Wolfe for her White Chocolate Cream Cheese Filled Chocolate Cupcakes." Applause thundered in my ears as I hesitated, not sure I had heard correctly. It was true though; I had won first place. My knees were weak as I walked through the crowd to receive the big blue ribbon rosette. On the way, I had to dodge all the daggers that were being thrown my way from the looks some of the losers were giving me. Better luck next year, ladies.

I really was proud of myself. I don't win very often. I called everyone I could think of that would care: Mom, Sandy, and Jamie. Not a single one of them believed me. Jamie even asked me when I was going to tell the judges I had bought the cupcakes from the grocery store. Butthead.

This started a yearly quest for me. I am normally not a competitive person. I learned that from Mom. Attending a small Catholic school in a small town didn't help. We weren't exactly perennial powerhouses in any sport when I was growing up. Suffering a major defeat was met with, "Well somebody had to lose," as a consolation from Mom. If the game had been competitive and our team came up short by a point or two, Mom would say, "That's not losing. That's bad luck."

I have discovered my inner competitive monster though in the baking contest. I have become one of those cutthroat bitches who expect to win every year.

And I do.

Following my victory with the cupcakes, I took first place with my chocolate chip cookies. The next year I won with a Lemon Berry Tart or, as my stepdaughter refers to it, Orgasm on a Fork. Unfortunately, I had to sit out the following year because I was still recovering from the hysterectomy I had to remove a tumor the size of a softball.

I decided to make my triumphant return to the baking contest with my Triple Layer Chocolate Cake with an almond chocolate icing that is so good it makes you want to smear it all over someone and then lick it off. Mmmmmmm, my mouth is watering.

The big day arrived. The cake was baked to perfection. The icing was as sin inducing as ever. I was ready.

Off I went, speeding down the road because, just like having to pee, I am always late. I was within a half a mile of the fairgrounds when a tractor pulled out in front of me.

Screeeeeech!

Not good. Not good at all… the cake flew off the seat, smashed into the dashboard, and plopped on the floor.

No, no, no, no, no, I thought to myself, this did NOT just happen. My cake! My beautiful cake! My guaranteed first place cake! It was an absolute heap of chocolate covered in dirt, rocks, and dog hairs from the car floor.

Because the competitive bitch monster was already loose, just going home was not an option.

I'll just go back home, make another batch of icing and put this thing back together, I plotted. I can scrape off the worst parts, fill in the holes, build it back up, and cover it with sprinkles.

I was not going to admit defeat. No way. No how. I was determined. I was focused. I was going to win, damn it!

Piecing together what ingredients I had left, I managed to eek out a half a batch of icing to work with.

Voila!

Perfection. Sorta.

I stood back, admired my handy work, and then needed to go to the bathroom. Of course. Now, it does *not* take that long to go to the bathroom. What, two, three minutes tops? The thought that anything else could possibility go wrong just seemed nonexistent. Actually, the thought that anything else could go wrong never even entered my mind. Ha.

I returned to the kitchen to find that Jinx, my black cat, had jumped up on the counter and licked his way around the entire cake.

Are you kidding me with this?

Throwing in the towel was still not an option. Throwing on more sprinkles was. Lots of sprinkles.

The cake took second place.

Now if that's not a testament to my baking skills that my Triple Layer Chocolate Cake with Dirt, Rock, Dog Hairs, Licked-by-a-Cat Icing can still take second place, I don't know what is.

Except my award winning Salted Caramel Cashew Tarts.

***

As a high school teacher working in an urban school district, I sometimes wonder if I have actually died and am now in Hell, serving my punishment and just don't realize it.

Since I wasn't exactly a model, straight "A" student like Smart-as-a-Whip Sandy or even a quiet, mediocre student like Don't-Even-Know-I'm-In-The-Room Dan, I am sure this calling is God's twisted answer to my prayers of me not wanting to be a nun. For me to end up back in a classroom despite all those parent-teacher conferences and torturous Sunday nights when I was a student is very ironic.

Oh that God, He sure is funny.

No, since I was that student who was ornery, talkative, and just smart enough to get decent grades without having to really work hard it, I have been blessed with the same type of students.

Haha, Miss Karma, good one.

If I had been smart when I first started teaching I would have kept a journal of all the unbelievable incidents and events that I have experienced. A compilation of that magnitude would have either gotten me fired or made me rich.

Where to start?

I've been slammed in a doorway with the door, called every name in the book, and have had my purse, cell phone, fans, electric pencil sharpener, and watch stolen. I have witnessed more fistfights and arrests than I care to recall. There is no air conditioning in my classroom but when I installed window air conditioners myself, I was written up and a permanent letter was put in my file. I have had soggy ceiling tiles collapse onto my desk while I was grading papers due to water damage from a leaky roof. I've removed bats, bugs, and mice from my room. I have been accused of being a racist.

I have also met some amazing young people who were trying their best to do the right thing. Some failed but so many more have succeeded.

Because teaching is a great deal more exhausting and stressful than a large majority of people think, we all have different ways of relieving our tensions. Mine is exercise. In addition to walking the dogs after school, I used to take walks on my lunch break. Used to.

One lovely spring day I headed out to do my usual loop around the neighborhood. This included walking past a middle school. On this fateful afternoon I saw three boys sneak out a side door who then nervously yet thoroughly checked around the corner of the building to see if anyone was watching, and finally broke out into a run, jubilant in their truancy. Because I was too far away to immediately do anything, I instead laughed to myself, feeling a sort of kindred spirit with these fellow rule breakers.

Well, wouldn't you know, a couple of blocks later, here came that same trio, walking straight toward me. Because I was still feeling an unspoken camaraderie toward them, I thought I'd be the better person by stepping into the grass and letting the boys have the sidewalk. No sooner had they passed me than one of them turned around and yelled, "Hey, bitch! I gotta gun! I'm gonna cap yo' ass!"

Maybe it was the teacher in me or maybe it was the repressed redneck in me trying to get out but instead of just ignoring them and walking away, like a mature adult would have done, I turned around, put my hands on my hips, squared up my shoulders, and narrowed my eyes to a seething glare. Then very deliberately I looked to my left and then to my right and then straight at the little snot-nosed pubescent brats. In a deep, strict, hard-ass, albeit incredulous, voice I rumbled, "WHO ARE YOU TALKING

TO? I KNOW YOU'RE NOT TALKING TO ME!"

I fully expected them to hightail it out of there as fast as they could. This was Ms. Wolfe they were dealing with. Nobody talks to Wolfie like that.

"We're talking to you, bitch! We're gonna put a cap in yo' white ass!"

"Yeah, Cracker! You better run! This is my street!"

"We're gonna fuck you up, whitey!"

Oh no they didn't. Oh no they didn't just say that to me. To me? Hmph.

The mature adult in me was too stunned to react appropriately so the juvenile delinquent in me gleefully stepped in. In a crazed fashion, I thumped my fists on my chest, raised my arms out to the side, and bellowed back, "Take your best shot, mother fuckers! Come on! That's right! I said take your best shot!"

Seeing a deranged, sweaty woman challenging them to bring it on must have been the catalyst for their hasty retreat. Still angry, I started stomping my way back to school, all the while muttering darkly to myself, "Just who do they think they are talking to me like that? If they only knew who they were dealing with. Punk ass little kids! And here I thought it was funny they were ditching school. Threatening me with a gun. 'Cap yo' ass,' my ass!..."

Hmmm.

With this last thought came another thought: What if the reason they ran away so fast was so that they *could* go get a gun and then come back...

Now I was the one hightailing it back to school. Please, God, please don't let me get shot! Don't let me get shot out here all alone! Just help me until I get on school grounds! Just let me get to the parking lot and then they can shoot me! Jamie will need the insurance money!

See, if I get hurt or killed on school grounds, there will actually be some compensation. If not, well, too bad. So in my frantic state of mind, I was more concerned as to where I got gunned down instead of actually being gunned down. I have really good insurance.

Sprinting is not something I was good at even at a younger age. Trying to sprint three blocks without tripping and falling down, praying that I make it back to school as a middle-aged, gin drinking high school teacher was a monumental achievement. When I finally reached the parking lot, I bent over and gasped for air.

Wheezing a bit, I started to laugh. I just knew I would eventually end up with those boys in my class some day.

***

I didn't get shot that day but Miss Karma thought I needed some payback for cussing at middle schoolers. I personally think this was unfair of Karma.

They started it.

Karma's retribution began with a fight over two dollars in the school cafeteria. The accused two dollar hoarder, Wallace, just happened to be a student in my next period class. When the bell was about to ring, the two instigators, James and Denzel, followed him to my room. Because I had James in class the year before, I told him to just drop it and go to class. If it was that big of a deal to him and his buddy, I would just give them the two dollars myself.

That wasn't the point. James and Denzel needed to save face. Because they had been shooting their mouths off so much in the cafeteria, talking trash about how they were going to give it to Wallace, a large crowd had followed them upstairs. Listening to a teacher by turning around and leaving without finishing what they had started just wasn't going to cut it.

That wasn't cool. That wasn't tough. That wasn't gangsta.

So, as I was standing in the doorway, just about to yell to everyone to go to class and get out of the hallway, James made his move. He "football" tackled me- like when a receiver has the football and he needs to get past a defender, he lowers his head, using it and his shoulders to bust past the opponent- causing me to lose my footing.

Now, if I had just fallen down, I would have landed on my butt and would have been spared serious injury due to the cushioning my backside would have provided.

That wasn't cool. That wasn't tough. That wasn't coordinated.

No, no, I needed to prove how gangsta I was by trying to stay on my feet, backpedaling to keep my balance. This wasn't the best idea: I crashed into my heavy wooden desk head first, knocking myself silly.

As if it wasn't bad enough to have been nearly knocked out in my own classroom by my own desk, as I lay on the floor trying to get my wits about me, students that were in the hallway came rushing in the room to get a ringside view of the action and were literally stepping on me to gain access. Stepping. On. Me.

I was so pissed off and, as everyone knows by now, when I get pissed off, you are going to hear about it.

"ALRIGHT! That is ENOUGH! I want everyone out of my room RIGHT NOW or I'm going to..."

Nobody got to find out what exactly I was going to do because all of the sudden-

WHACK!

WHAM!

THUD!

Someone had thrown a desk and right as I got to my feet it hit me, throwing me backwards into the chalkboard, again hitting my head. I also managed to hit my lower back on the chalk ledge which caused one of those nausea inducing pains like when you stub your toe. I hate that.

Man, oh, man. Things were just going from bad to worse. It was right about this time that I decided the situation had gotten just a little too out of control even for Ms. Wolfe and that perhaps I should try to get some assistance. Getting some assistance turned out to be more complicated than I thought because by now an extremely large crowd had gathered in the hallway outside my room. No one was coming in or going out. One of my teacher friends, Mr. Becker, told me later that he and several other teachers had tried to reach me but couldn't get through the growing crowd. Crazy, I know.

Still in teacher mode and banking on my notoriety as Ms. Wolfe, I thought for sure someone would help so imagine the face-slapping surprise I felt when no one listened to me or tried to help me. This wasn't fun or funny.

Since standing in the doorway yelling at whoever would listen had worked so well for me when this whole catastrophe started, I thought using that same tactic would somehow make the situation better now. So, as I was standing in the doorway, just about to yell for someone, anyone, to go get a damn administrator and get the hell out of my way, I noticed the fight had worked its way back to the front of the classroom. I turned around with every intention of trying to get out of the way but because I am slow and white, I wasn't fast enough. With Wallace standing in between us, Denzel cocked his arm back and threw a haymaker at him.

I grew up in the country in the middle of nowhere. I went to a Catholic school. I have an older brother who had big friends.

Needless to say, I was not experienced in street fighting.

But Wallace was.

He ducked. I didn't.

WHAM!

WHACK!

THUD!

Denzel's fist nailed me right on the chin, sending me flying out the door. I landed on the very hard, very cold tile floor. Oomph.

I'm not sure how many times my head bounced off the floor but when I finally slid to a stop, my head came to rest at the feet of a student who seemed to be peering down on me from ten feet up. I just remember looking at this guy and thinking to myself, "That is the biggest student I have ever seen. How is it that I don't know who he is?" Turned out, it was Jared Sullinger, one of our school's basketball players. He was a freshman at the time and he wasn't in any of my classes so I had somehow missed his 6'9" frame walking the hallways. But since my notoriety knows no bounds, he knew who I was.

"Ms. Wolfe! Ms. Wolfe! Are you alright?" he asked towering over me.

"Don't worry Ms. Wolfe! I'll help you!" Jared assured me, leaning down, grabbing me by the front of my shirt and pulling me up off the ground. Using a football tackle similar to the one that started this whole thing, he tucked me under one arm and used his other arm to plow through the unrelenting crowd until we reached the edge of the mob, where he unceremoniously plunked me back on my feet.

By now the school police officer and several building administrators had arrived, clearing out the mob and apprehending James and Denzel. Mr. Becker and the building principal, Mr. Smith, showed up to ask me what had happened. I related the events to them the best that I could remember. They kept asking me if I was okay and if I wanted to go to the emergency room. Because I have the reputation of being Ms. Wolfe to uphold, I kept telling them I was fine and that I had a class to teach.

"My head is starting to hurt, though," I muttered, reaching to feel the back of my head only to touch something slimy, warm, and thick.

"Ewww! Someone spit on me!" I exclaimed, bringing my hand back around to my face. Hitting my head three or four times really hard had caused a little confusion for me so when I saw that my hand was covered in blood instead of a lugey, it took a minute for me to figure out that despite my natural hard headedness, I was actually injured.

This was later confirmed in the emergency room. I first realized something was wrong when, being handed a clip board with some paperwork that needed to be signed, I couldn't remember my name. When I just sat there, staring at the paper like it was some unsolvable calculus problem, the nurse sort of looked at me and again told me to sign on the bottom line.

"Well, I will, just as soon as I can remember my name," I flippantly replied, trying to play off this mental lapse as coolly as I could. Hello, Embarrassment! I was wondering where you had been!

The nurse patted me on the knee, told me she was going to get the doctor, and left the room with one last uncertain look at me over her shoulder. Damn. I must really be in bad shape, I thought to myself.

Being in bad shape turned out to be a couple of fractured vertebrae, a cracked tailbone, several torn muscles, and a level three concussion.

But don't you fret. You know Ms. Karma's got my back. James ended up in jail. Denzel was shot and killed running down a back alleyway during a drug deal gone bad. As for Jared, he was awarded a full scholarship to play basketball at the Ohio State University after winning our school's first boy's State Championship in over 20 years.

What comes around goes around. Amen to that, sister.

6

SIX

"There's no place like home. There's no place like home."

-Dorothy, from *The Wizard of Oz*

"I would rather have a nod from an American than a snuff-box from an emperor."
-Lord Byron

"You should take a vacation," Jamie's aunt was saying. "Take a week. It would be nice for the two of you to get away and relax."

Get away, relax. Sure.

I am a homebody. I'm not a big fan of flying. I get car sick. I don't like change. Jamie on the other hand, loves traveling around, experiencing new places and people. Not me. I would much rather lounge on the dock and read a book. Or lounge in front of a small bonfire, drinking a gin and tonic. That is vacation enough for me but because Jamie considers my lack of wanderlust a character flaw, every once in a while I will believe him when he tells me I am missing out on all kinds of grand adventures. So, after deciding on a location, I spent the next six months repeating my unsuccessful camping mantra, "I will have fun on this trip. I will have fun on this trip. I will have fun…"

This fun trip was to Margarita Island, a supposed resort locale off the coast of Venezuela. According to the travel brochures, it is quite popular among European vacationers.

See that red flag over there? The one that says two Americans who don't speak Spanish traveling to Venezuela is not a good idea? Yeah, that one. Yeah, we missed it too.

Margarita Island is actually one of Dante's levels of hell; which level, I am not sure, but it has to be damn close to the bottom.

Day One started when we excitedly left our house at 5:30 A.M. for a "trip of a lifetime." Oh it turned out to be unforgettable, that's for sure. First, I was pulled out of line at the airport by uniformed TSA agents to have my luggage emptied and inspected while I stood spread eagle, being patted down and "wanded". There is nothing like standing in a plexiglass box at 6 A.M. in the middle of the airport, feeling like the proverbial car wreck- everyone was staring at me while avoiding eye contact, craning their necks to watch as they freely moved along. I kept a feeling of panic at bay by thinking to myself, "I will have fun on this trip. I will have fun on this trip."

Next, our flight from Miami to Venezuela was delayed by four hours, causing us to miss our connecting flight to the island, thereby missing our arranged hook-up with a tour guide.

We didn't think it would be a problem until we arrived. There we discovered practically no one spoke English or was willing to speak English to us.

It was a total nightmare. People can put down Americans and say we are rude but if the treatment we received in the customs line at this airport is an example of the rest of the world's version of politeness, then that particular line of political correctness is bullshit. We were either ignored, ditched, pushed, or glared at until we finally made it through only to be left in the lobby of a nearly empty "international airport" where there wasn't one single airline/airport employee who could speak English. Really? Isn't English considered to be the international language?

Luckily, a fellow passenger took pity on us and was willing to help us out. She explained that because we had missed the last connecting flight to the island, the airline was putting us up in a hotel for the night. And then she left. We were on our own.

The "hotel" we were taken to barely qualified as livable, let alone a hotel. Webster's defines a hotel as "a house for entertaining strangers or travelers; an inn or public house, of the better class"; better class, my ass. We spent the night with our clothes on, the lights on, and one eye on the locked and bolted door.

On Day Two, we finally arrived on the island and were able to track down our English-speaking tour guide, Herman. He arranged for a taxi to take us to our resort, scheduled some activities for the next day, and then left, telling us to enjoy the rest of the day.

Enjoy the rest of the day. Insert derisive snort here.

First we had to endure a 40 minute cab ride driven by a surly man who didn't seem too keen about driving a couple of Americans around but who was very keen on Jesus. People have funny ways about Jesus. This taxicab was plastered from hood to rear bumper with decals and stickers of varying images of Jesus. The interior was festively adorned with more stickers, along with rosaries and plastic statues. Even the seat covers had Jesus on them. I'm not sure what Father Paul would say, but, in my opinion, sitting on Jesus' face is just not right.

No matter, I told myself. We are finally here, on the beach, ready to have fun on this trip. Snort.

Apparently, God didn't think having Jesus' nose stuffed up my ass was right either because I paid for my butt faux pas through public humiliation. We weren't on the beach more than an hour when some French guy felt we were crowding in on his beach territory. Apparently he thought I was trying to steal his beach chair because he started yelling loud enough for the whole beach to hear, "You Americans are all the same! Always trying to take over everything!" Yes, Frenchy, that's right. We Americans are embarking on world domination one lounge chair at a time.

How fun! The proverbial car wreck has moved to the Autobahn!

Day Three was the day I was convinced would be the start of our fun. It was the first day with our English-speaking tour guide, Herman, who drove like a maniac while drinking rum and Coke. Lots of rum and Coke. After describing yesterday's fiasco at the resort beach, Herman took us to a lesser-known public beach away from the resort. It didn't take long for trouble to catch up with us again. What was it with these beach chairs? Apparently, the beach chair rental guy thought we were stiffing him- not because we used chairs without paying for them but because we didn't rent any chairs at all, choosing to sit on towels in the sand. Oy vey.

We decided that maybe the beach scene wasn't for us and instead chose to do some sightseeing and shopping. Pearls and hand-made pottery are the big commodities on Margarita Island because they are cheap and abundant.

Because I always have to pee, it didn't take long for all those rum and Cokes to catch up with me. So at the first pottery shop, I asked Herman to ask the shop owner if she had a restroom I could use. Smiling politely, she walked me through the gift shop, past one restroom, into the workshop, passing another restroom, through the warehouse, passing a third restroom, out to the garbage dump at the very back of the property, where, while still smiling (bitch), she pointed to a spot on the ground near a rusty refrigerator. Really, lady? You can't be bothered to show a smidgen of hospitality to a stranger in a strange place (who, by the way, was willing to spend money in your store) by letting me relieve myself with dignity? Instead, you want me to pop a squat on the ground, behind a rusty refrigerator, in a trash dump. Nice. I had to pee too bad to argue. Needless to say, I didn't get to wash my hands either.

The fun had better start soon.

Day 4 was a Tuesday. The travel brochures said Margarita Island has 340 days of sunshine a year. That leaves 25 rainy days. Tuesday was one of them. Fortunately, it only rained in the morning so our trip to the mangroves with Leah and Mike, the only other Americans we encountered in 7 days, wasn't ruined. Yet.

That was accomplished by the captains who refused to rent a boat to our group.

"No Negroes! No Negroes!" we were told, referring to Mike. I have to hand it to Mike. He handled the situation like a gentleman. Not wanting to spend the rest of my life wasting away in some third world prison shit hole where no one ever hears from me again, I kept my mouth shut too.

Until later.

I think Herman felt bad about the way Mike was treated so he took us out to eat at a restaurant that served dinner on the beach. Everyone had a few more rum and Cokes and started to relax. We even struck up a conversation with the group of diners at the next table. One of the women was some kind of expatriate who spent the last twenty years living in Paris and had just recently returned to her wonderful homeland. I figured that explained the reason why someone her size and age was still trying to stuff herself into a gold bikini that was at least two sizes too small. Maybe her mirror hadn't arrived from France yet.

I'm not sure where it all started to go wrong. One minute we were all enjoying the sunset, the next minute their group got some kind of burr up their asses. The expatriate lady started spouting off in Spanish, ending her tirade with a nasty sneer on her face as she spat out, "DUR-TY A-MARY-CAANS!"

Dirty Americans?

This time is was definitely the redneck in me that jumped up along with Jamie, Mike, and Herman.

"Ha! I'd rather be a 'dur-ty A-mary-caan' than a Nazi sympathizer! AND, if it wasn't for us 'dur-ty A-mary-caans', you and your little French friends would be speaking German!" I spat back at her, preparing to bob and weave. I wanted to be able to duck this time. Fortunately there weren't any desks to be thrown and before anyone could grab chairs, the manager threw out the durty Amarycaan haters.

So much for Tuesday.

Day Five didn't bring any improvement in our quest for fun. The one good thing about Wednesday was the fact that Venezuelans only had to endure 23 more rainy days. It was pouring buckets when we woke up and slowed to an on-and-off drizzle the rest of the day. Again, we couldn't find a boat captain who was willing to take us out snorkeling and sightseeing. We eventually ended up on a foul beachfront where the local fishermen brought in and cleaned their catch. And I mean they literally gutted and cleaned their fish in the water. The water was filthy. I'm not sure what was worse: the nauseating smell of dead fish or seeing fish heads, guts, and other fish parts floating around in the water.

Herman managed to hire a drunken Brazilian fisherman who was moored for the day and didn't mind making a few bucks off of some tourists. This guy seemed happy enough. Decked out in what appeared to be trashcan liner fashioned into a raincoat, he didn't mind the rain, the Americans, or the smell. He serenaded us with song as he piloted his boat out to the island we were going to snorkel around. I have to admit, despite the cold rain and fish guts, the snorkeling was a success. The exotic underwater plant life and the differently colored fish were beautiful.

Finally some fun. And then Canada showed up.

After Herman dropped off Jamie and I at our hotel we were exhausted from dodging fish guts while snorkeling and practicing karaoke with an inebriated Brazilian fisherman, so we headed to the buffet line at the resort dining hall. As Jamie went to find a table, I stood in line. Suddenly, I heard what seemed to be angels sent from heaven: the couple in front of me was speaking perfect English!

Americans!

Without thinking, I blurted out, "You're Americans, too?"

If the look Lewis shot me questioned whether or not I was the Devil in disguise, the glare this guy gave me confirmed it beyond a doubt.

Recoiling from me, he sniffed, "I would never be an American. We are from Canada."

Okay, that's cool. I like Canada.

"Well then, we're practically neighbors," I added cheerfully, trying to save face, "Since we don't speak Spanish, it's been hard having conversations with the other guests. So when I heard you talking, you sounded so American."

"Maybe you should have learned the language before traveling here," he huffed.

Well no shit, Sherlock. Look dude, enough with the attitude. You're from Canada. Canada. I mean, come on.

Since I don't know when to keep my mouth shut most times, I bumbled on, trying to fix the situation.

"So what part of Canada are you from?"

"We are from Quebec." Ahhhh, that explains a lot: *French* Canadians. Jamie warned me about them after he went caribou hunting in Northern Quebec. Hell, not even other Canadians like French Canadians.

For a fleeting moment, I considered introducing him to Frenchy from the beach but decided against it. I was afraid the cloud of smug they would create would block out the sun, ending life as we know it.

Day Six. Oh boy, Day 6. What a day it turned into. It was, once again, raining, which really sucked for us because we had booked ourselves onto a catamaran tour boat that traveled from Margarita Island to a ring of smaller islands a few miles offshore. When it really started to rain hard, all the other passengers headed below deck. Jamie and I tried to squeeze in too but no one seemed to want to make room for us dur-ty A-mary-caans so we sat on deck. In the rain. All by ourselves. I just couldn't handle all the fun we were having.

Finally, a young couple from Finland came up and sat with us. Apparently, people from Finland don't have a problem with Americans because they were actually willing to interact with us. So too was the older couple from Israel. Of all the people we encountered, these Israelis were definitely the most interesting and entertaining. Talk about a pair of characters. Their son went to Notre Dame University. Yes, *that* Notre Dame. Oh believe me, we all got a kick out of the irony of an Israeli Jewish student attending a very Catholic university.

It was nice having some allies on the boat because the French couple and German mother and daughter were not friendly at all. When I tried to empathize with the daughter, who was green with motion sickness, her mother came over, grabbed her by the wrist, and yanked her across the boat, as far away from us as she could get. Sprechen Sie Deutsch?

The French couple turned their noses up at us all day until it was time to eat and they were forced to sit next to us. Jamie, ever the diplomat, clumsily tried to make conversation with them in French (he studied it in high school and was a little rusty). For whatever reason, this impressed them enough to lower themselves to talk to us.

After that, besides the Germans, the day went swimmingly well thanks to the rum punch that was served by the first mate. This drink was so unbelievably delicious; it went down way too easy. By the end of the day, everyone, including the captain of the boat, was extremely intoxicated and very happy about it. Well, I'm not sure about the Germans, but then again, after an incalculable number of drinks, I wasn't sure about anything, except never try to drink a red-colored liquid while wearing light colored clothes on a large sailboat bouncing over rough water.

We were really drunk.

After docking and disembarking, we all said goodbye to each other with sloppy hugs and uncoordinated handshakes. We were the last to leave because we were waiting on Herman. This was bad for us- very bad. Just like with the rum and Cokes, the rum punch had reached our kidneys with an unexpected speed and urgency. Feigning sobriety, we walked around with as much dignity as we could muster, trying to find a restroom. There wasn't a single one to be found.

Since I had already suffered the degradation of having to pop a squat in a trash dump, peeing in my bathing suit while sitting in a grassy strip as I pretended to be tying my shoes was nothing for me. For Jamie, however, this was another matter altogether. But just like the strange effects of motion sickness, the rum punch must have addled his sensibility. As he stood a few feet next to me, he peed down his leg all the while carrying on a conversation with me as if it were perfectly normal to pee on yourself out in public. It was the only time I was glad that there were 25 rainy days in Venezuela.

Day 7 will forever be known as Black Friday. It was the stuff of nightmares. Some of my worst fears all converged in a single day: fishing, fish, motion sickness, being hot and sweaty, and puking.

Jamie wanted to go deep sea fishing. Because I love and adore my husband to no end, I agreed to go with him. Herman told us that the cove we would be fishing in would be as smooth as glass and that I shouldn't have to worry about getting seasick.

That would have been all fine and dandy if it hadn't, for the fourth straight day, been raining. Not wanting to lose the deposit for our "seats" on the fishing boat, we headed out. I've seen fishing boat tours and I had a certain idea of what to expect.

What's that old saying, hope for the best while expecting the worst? I needed to drop my expectations really, really low. Really low. Keep going. A little lower. I'll tell you when to stop.

Our deep sea fishing boat was just that: a 16-foot wooden V-hall boat with rickety boards for the seven of us dumb asses to sit on. No lifejackets. No fishing poles. No rum punch. The guys used steel wire wrapped around their hands to fish with. As traditional as Jamie is with his hunting equipment, this was a little much even for him.

Due to the storms during the night, the smooth as glass water was roiling with six to eight foot waves. At first, it wasn't so bad. As we headed out to sea, it was like riding a roller coaster going up and down, up and down. It wasn't until we reached our designated fishing spot when the boat pilot turned the boat sideways that I began to have trouble. The boat was now being rocked in the swells from side to side.

I lasted about 5 minutes.

I have experienced many levels and types of motion sickness. This was by far the worst I have ever felt and that's saying something. If Venezuela is one of the lowest levels of Hell, sitting in that fishing boat was *the* lowest. It was awful. I thought I was dying.

To add to my misery was the actual fishing itself. They didn't use poles. They used metal line that Jamie had to wrap around his hand. Visions of Jamie's hand being sliced off flashed into my mind, occasionally blocking out my focus on the horizon which I was intently staring at to try to alleviate my nausea and get my vomiting to stop.

Finally, Jamie hooked a fish. Thank you, Jesus. Now we could head back to shore. My persecution would be over.

But wait, it gets better.

When Jamie pulled the fish into the boat, it was a pinfish, kind of like a miniature marlin with the pointy snout. The fishing guide grabbed it with his bare hands and then, with a grinding sound I can still hear in my head, snapped its head off. But of course, since fish are freaky, even though it *had* to be dead, it continued to flop around in the dirty water that had collected in the bottom of the boat.

I just couldn't see how any of this could get any worse.

Oh silly woman.

This is me we're talking about here.

Of course things can get worse.

They can *always* get worse.

And get worse it did.

After the vomit fest on the fishing boat, all I had to do was get through 12 more hours. 12 more hours and the vacation from hell would be over. I would be on American soil. I would be home.

12 hours.

I planned to sleep through at least six of them. Instead, I spent the next 12 hours with food poisoning. 12 hours of experiencing the joys of having bodily fluids come out at both ends at the same time. What a wonderful end to such a wonderful week with such wonderful people.

Since Day Eight started the same way Day Seven had ended, my one focus was packing and going home. I just wanted to go home.

But of course it couldn't be that easy.

Herman picked us up bright and early to drive us to the airport. I somehow managed the 40 minute ride with only puking out the window and not needing to change my drawers. As we stood waiting to board the plane, we were pulled out of line. We were soon joined by a Japanese tourist, an African man, and a family from Cuba. Again, since Devil's Island is so worldly, there were no employees who could speak English, let alone Japanese. The Cuban grandfather explained to us that the jumper flight was overbooked and that we had been bumped to a later flight.

Hmph. Strange. Only foreigners were bumped.

Hmph.

I guess Americans weren't the only dur-ty tourists on the island. I'll give the Venezuelans this much: at least they're equal opportunity haters. They seem to hate everyone equally.

Four hours later we were finally flying back to the mainland. Another hour after that we were headed for Miami. Miss Karma must have come back from being At The Grocery Store because redemption was coming.

Miami International Airport has two sections for customs: one for Americans, one for everybody else. Despite my Catholic guilt, I just couldn't help but indulge in some self-satisfaction as we breezed through the American section while long lines formed in the Everybody Else section. It was packed. I missed you so much, Karma!

7

Afterword

"It is not true that life is one damn thing after another... It's one damn thing over and over."

-Edna St. Vincent Millay

My life continues on in its own unique fashion. It is still not boring.

Today I went to Home Depot and went through the U-Scan it line. The money machine kept my change.

Next I went to Chipotle. I paid for my lunch with a twenty but the cashier gave me back change for a ten. When I pointed it out to her that she had given me the wrong change, she gave me a nasty look and told me that I should get out of line instead of trying to scam her out of money.

After that, I had a bikini wax. Fun.

Arriving home, I started pulling weeds only to be sent screaming into the house after several yellow jackets flew up my shorts and stung me on my freshly waxed, um, how can I put this delicately? My freshly waxed girly parts.

Really- who else do you know that would get stung on their privates?

Karma must have been following as closely as the bees were.

First off, the manager from the Home Depot called to let me know that after running the tape from the cash register, he had found my transaction and wanted to remedy the situation by reimbursing me the cost of my purchased items.

Secondly, the manager from the Chipotle called to apologize. She rectified the situation by not only reimbursing me my money back but issuing me gift cards and firing the cashier.

Lastly, and most importantly, I looked fantastic in my swimsuit at the lake party.

Published by FastPencil
http://www.fastpencil.com

Tony Marconi holds undergraduate degrees in history and sociology from Southern Illinois University and a Master's in Education from George Washington University. He is a retired special needs educator, a member of the North Unitarian Universalist Congregation in Lewis Center, Ohio, and a long-time advocate and activist for socio-economic justice issues in general and LGBTQ rights in particular.

Tony served as an active member and chairperson of the Delaware Gay Straight Christian Alliance, and, along with his life partner, Martha, was part of a coalition of representatives that helped found Equality Ohio. He served on the Board of Directors for Equality Ohio, and in his "spare time" gave lectures on the subject of homosexuality and the Bible.

Tony is still available for free lectures and group discussions on this topic, and may be contacted at: tonymartha@columbus.rr.com